HOW TO BUILD A WEALTHIER FUTURE AND A HAPPIER RELATIONSHIP

Christian Wolf

Mary Fiorentino

DEDICATION

To Luke and Peter, our beloved sons. This book is dedicated to you, the brightest stars in our universe. As we embark on this journey, we want you to know that you are our greatest inspiration. May the wisdom and insights within these pages guide you towards a future filled with financial prosperity, harmonious relationships, and boundless happiness.

CONTENTS

1 UNITED BY FINANCE: AN INTRODUCTION

In every relationship, there are different factors that contribute to its success. Trust, communication, love, and respect are usually at the top of the list. However, there's one factor that couples often overlook: financial compatibility. It's been said that money is the root of many disagreements, and it can even lead to breakups. But what if money could be a uniting force instead of a dividing one? That's what this book, and this chapter, is all about. Welcome to "United by Finance".

Money is not just about dollars and cents. It's about values, priorities, goals, and dreams. When a couple is financially compatible, they see eye-to-eye on these critical aspects of life. They have a shared vision for their future and a common plan to get there. They communicate openly about money, make financial decisions together, and support each other in achieving their financial goals.

However, achieving financial compatibility isn't always easy. It requires honesty, openness, compromise, and mutual respect. It requires a shared commitment to financial responsibility and a willingness to work together toward shared goals. It's not about having the same amount of money or earning the same income. It's about having a shared understanding of the role of money in your lives and a shared approach to managing it.

In this chapter, we're going to explore the concept of financial compatibility in more depth. We'll look at why it's so important, how to achieve it, and the benefits it can bring to your relationship.

Why Financial Compatibility Matters

Many couples shy away from talking about money, especially early in the relationship. It's often seen as a taboo topic, something that's too personal or potentially divisive to discuss. However, avoiding the topic of money can lead to misunderstandings, disagreements, and resentment down the line.

In contrast, couples who are financially compatible have open, honest conversations about money. They understand each other's financial habits, attitudes, and goals. They know where they stand financially, both individually and as a couple, and they make financial decisions together.

Financial compatibility is crucial because it affects so many aspects of a couple's life together. It impacts your lifestyle, your stress levels, your ability to achieve your goals, and your sense of security and stability. When a couple is financially compatible, they're better equipped to navigate the financial ups and downs of life together. They're more likely to be satisfied with their financial situation and less likely to argue about money.

How to Achieve Financial Compatibility

Achieving financial compatibility is a process. It doesn't happen overnight, and it requires ongoing effort and communication. Here are some steps to help you and your partner become more financially compatible:

1. **Open the Lines of Communication**: Start by having open, honest conversations about money. Discuss your financial histories, attitudes, habits, and goals. Understand where each other is coming from and where you want to go.

2. **Create a Shared Budget**: A shared budget can help you align your spending with your shared goals. It can also make it easier to manage your money together and keep track of your progress.

3. **Set Shared Goals**: What do you want to achieve together, financially? Whether it's buying a house, starting a family, traveling the world, or saving for retirement, having shared goals can motivate you to work together and keep your financial habits aligned.

4. **Support Each Other**: Financial compatibility is not just about the practical side of managing money. It's also about the emotional support you give each other. Be there for each other during financial challenges and celebrate each other's financial successes.

The Benefits of Financial Compatibility

Financial compatibility can bring numerous benefits to your relationship. It can reduce financial stress, promote better communication, and foster a deeper sense of trust and intimacy.

When you're financially compatible, you're more likely to feel secure and stable in your relationship. You're less likely to argue about money and more likely to feel satisfied with your financial situation. You're more likely to achieve your financial goals and to enjoy the journey along the way.

In conclusion, financial compatibility is a critical aspect of a successful, happy relationship. It's about more than just money—it's about shared values, goals, and dreams. It's about working together to build the life you want. We hope this chapter has given you a deeper understanding of the importance of financial compatibility and inspired you to strive for it in your own relationship.

In every successful relationship, there are various factors that contribute to happiness and harmony. Trust, communication, love, and respect often top the list. However, one crucial factor that couples often overlook is financial compatibility. Money has the potential to be a unifying force instead of a dividing one. When couples are financially compatible, they share a deep understanding of the role of money in their lives and work together towards common goals. Financial compatibility brings happiness and harmony to the couple, allowing them to build a secure and fulfilling future together.

By fostering open communication, creating shared budgets, setting shared goals, and providing emotional support, couples can achieve financial compatibility and experience the joys it brings to their relationship. As we progress through this book, we will delve further into insights, strategies, and practical advice to help couples enhance their financial compatibility and strengthen their bond.

Remember, the journey to financial compatibility is not always easy, but the rewards are well worth the effort. As we continue through this book, we'll provide more insights, strategies, and practical advice to help you and your partner become more financially compatible. Stay tuned for Chapter 2, where we'll delve into the art of budgeting as a couple.

2 THE ART OF BUDGETING AS A COUPLE

Budgeting as a couple is an art. It's an intricate dance that combines financial realities with personal desires and future dreams. This chapter aims to equip you and your partner with the tools to make this dance more graceful and productive.

Understanding Budgeting Basics

Before delving into the specifics of budgeting as a couple, it's essential to understand the fundamentals of budgeting itself. In essence, budgeting is a process of balancing income (what you earn) with expenses (what you spend) to ensure you're living within your means and ideally saving for the future.

An effective budget should be realistic, flexible, and aligned with your financial goals. It's not about restricting your spending to the point of discomfort. Instead, it's about understanding where your money is going and making intentional decisions about how you want to use it.

Why Budget Together?

Budgeting together can strengthen your relationship and bring you closer as a couple. It promotes open and honest communication about money, helps align your financial goals, and encourages teamwork in managing your finances. It's an opportunity to understand each other's financial habits and preferences better and work together to make your money work for you.

Moreover, a shared budget can provide a clear picture of your joint financial health. It can highlight areas where you might be overspending and show opportunities to save more. It's a tool that can help you make informed decisions about your money and stay on track towards achieving your shared financial goals.

Starting the Budgeting Conversation

Initiating a conversation about money can be daunting, especially if it's a topic you've avoided in the past. But remember, this discussion is a crucial step towards financial compatibility and a healthier, happier relationship. Here are a few tips to get started:

1. **Choose the Right Time and Place**: Start the conversation at a time and place where you both feel relaxed and comfortable. Avoid times when either of you is stressed, tired, or distracted.

2. **Approach with Empathy**: Money can be an emotionally charged topic. Be mindful of each other's feelings and perspectives. Remember, the goal is not to blame or judge, but to understand and improve.

3. **Be Honest**: Be open and honest about your financial situation, habits, and goals. Honesty is the foundation of financial compatibility.

4. **Set Common Goals**: Discuss your shared dreams and aspirations. Whether it's buying a house, traveling the world, or saving for retirement, having common financial goals can provide motivation to stick to your budget.

Building Your Joint Budget

Once you've had the initial money conversation, the next step is to create your joint budget. Start by listing all sources of income (salary, investments, etc.) and all expenses (rent/mortgage, groceries, bills, etc.). Then, categorize your expenses into 'needs' (essential costs like housing, food, and healthcare) and 'wants' (non-essential but desired expenses like dining out, entertainment, etc.).

Next, allocate a specific portion of your income to each category, ensuring you're living within your means and saving for your goals. A common guideline is the 50/30/20 rule, where 50% of your income goes towards needs, 30% towards wants, and 20% towards savings. However, you can adjust these ratios based on your specific circumstances and goals.

Remember, creating a budget is just the first step. The real challenge lies in sticking to it. But don't worry, in the next part of this chapter, we'll discuss strategies for staying on track and making budgeting a shared responsibility.

Sticking to Your Joint Budget

Even the most meticulously planned budget can fall by the wayside if not adhered to consistently. Here are some practical tips for sticking to your budget:

1. **Regular Reviews**: Make it a habit to review your budget together at least once a month. This not only ensures you're on track but also allows for adjustments in case of any changes in your income, expenses, or financial goals.

2. **Be Flexible**: Understand that a budget isn't set in stone. There will be unexpected expenses, and there may be months where you overspend. The key is to adjust and adapt your budget as needed, rather than viewing these instances as failures.

3. **Use Tools and Apps**: Consider using budgeting tools or apps. Many of them allow you to track your expenses in real-time, send reminders for bill payments, and provide visual representations of your spending and saving habits.

4. **Celebrate Milestones**: Celebrating when you achieve a financial goal, no matter how small, can motivate you to keep going. It could be as simple as a special dinner at home or a small outing.

Dealing with Disagreements

It's natural to have disagreements when budgeting as a couple. Maybe one of you is a spender while the other is a saver. Perhaps you have different priorities when it comes to discretionary spending. Here's how you can navigate through these disagreements:

1. **Listen**: Before reacting, take the time to understand your partner's perspective. Their spending habits or viewpoints on money are likely shaped by their individual experiences and values.

2. **Compromise**: Find middle ground where both parties feel satisfied. For instance, if one partner loves dining out while the other prefers home-cooked meals to save money, you could agree on a set number of times to eat out each month.

3. **Maintain Some Independence**: While a joint budget is crucial for shared expenses and goals, having some independent money that each of you can spend as you wish can help reduce conflicts.

Creating a Savings Plan

Once you've built your budget, the next step is to create a joint savings plan. This plan should align with your shared financial goals, whether that's saving for a house, an annual vacation, or an emergency fund. Here's how to get started:

1. **Determine Your Goals**: Be clear about what you're saving for and why. Having a clear goal can provide motivation and make the act of saving more rewarding.

2. **Set a Timeline**: For each goal, determine a timeline. This helps you figure out how much you need to save each month to reach your goal in the desired timeframe.

3. **Automate Savings**: Consider setting up automatic transfers to your savings account. It's an easy way to ensure you're consistently contributing towards your goals without having to think about it.

4. **Consider Separate Accounts for Different Goals**: Having separate savings accounts for different goals can make it easier to track your progress and stay motivated.

When it comes to budget planning as a couple, the tool you use is not as important as the process itself. Whether you choose to use a budgeting app, a spreadsheet, or simply a notebook and a pen, what truly matters is the commitment and collaboration between partners. The elements that ideally should compose a couple's budget planning include:

1. **Income:** Determine your combined income from all sources, including salaries, investments, and side hustles.

2. **Expenses:** Track and categorize your expenses, including fixed expenses like rent or mortgage payments, utilities, transportation, groceries, and discretionary expenses like dining out, entertainment, and hobbies.

3. **Shared Financial Goals:** Identify and prioritize your shared financial goals, such as saving for a down payment, paying off debt, building an emergency fund, or planning for retirement.

4. **Individual Financial Goals:** Discuss and respect each other's individual financial goals, whether it's pursuing further education, starting a business, or supporting personal interests.

5. **Budget Categories:** Allocate appropriate amounts to different budget categories based on your priorities and financial responsibilities. This may

include savings, investments, debt repayment, and discretionary spending.

6. **Savings and Emergency Fund:** Set aside a portion of your income for savings and build an emergency fund to provide a safety net for unexpected expenses or financial setbacks.

7. **Debt Management:** Address any existing debts, such as student loans, credit card debt, or car loans. Prioritize debt repayment strategies based on interest rates and consider consolidating or refinancing if beneficial.

8. **Regular Budget Review:** Schedule regular check-ins to review your budget, track progress, and make necessary adjustments. This ensures you stay on track and adapt to any changes in your financial situation or goals.

9. **Open Communication:** Maintain open and honest communication about your financial situation, goals, and concerns. Discuss any potential conflicts or challenges that may arise and work together to find mutually beneficial solutions.

10. **Financial Accountability:** Hold each other accountable for adhering to the budget and making responsible financial decisions. Encourage and support each other in achieving your shared financial goals.

Here is a list outlining the main spending categories that should be included in a budget spreadsheet:

Spending Categories
Housing
Utilities
Transportation
Groceries
Dining Out
Entertainment
Health and Fitness
Insurance
Debt Payments
Savings and Investments
Personal Care
Education
Gifts and Donations
Travel
Miscellaneous

Remember, the key to successful budget planning as a couple lies in shared responsibility, transparency, and mutual respect. It's not about the tool you use, but the commitment to work together towards financial harmony and shared prosperity.

Conclusion

Budgeting as a couple is a journey that can strengthen your relationship and secure your financial future. It requires open communication, mutual understanding, compromise, and teamwork. But the rewards – increased financial stability, achievement of shared goals, reduced money-related stress, and a strengthened bond – are worth the effort.

Remember, the goal isn't to create a perfect budget, but a realistic one that serves your financial needs and dreams. As we move on to the next chapter, "Building a Strong Financial Foundation," we'll delve deeper into how to save, reduce debt, and invest wisely as a couple, all of which play crucial roles in turning your joint budget into a reality.

3 BUILDING A STRONG FINANCIAL FOUNDATION

Having laid out the importance of budgeting as a couple in the previous chapter, let's now turn our focus towards constructing a strong financial foundation. Building this base is a multi-faceted process, involving emergency funds, debt management, and long-term investments.

The Importance of a Strong Financial Foundation

A strong financial foundation provides you and your partner with the stability and security to withstand financial hiccups, realize long-term dreams, and live life on your terms. It's akin to building a house - a robust foundation ensures the house stands strong regardless of the storms it might face.

Creating this foundation isn't just about having money in the bank; it's about having a financial system in place that supports your current lifestyle and future ambitions. It involves having a safety net for emergencies, a plan for managing and eliminating debt, and a strategy for growing wealth through investments.

Creating an Emergency Fund

The first step in building your financial foundation is creating an emergency fund. This fund acts as a financial safety net, protecting you from unforeseen expenses like sudden medical bills, urgent car repairs, or job loss.

The general recommendation is to have three to six months' worth of living expenses saved in your emergency fund. This amount gives you the buffer to handle most financial emergencies without resorting to debt or dipping into your long-term savings.

Consider keeping your emergency fund in a high-yield savings account, where it remains accessible but also earns some interest. Automate monthly contributions to this account until you hit your target amount. Remember, an emergency fund is for emergencies only; refrain from tapping into it for non-urgent expenses.

Aligning on Debt Management

Debt can be a significant barrier to financial stability and growth. Thus, an essential part of your financial foundation is a shared strategy for managing and reducing debt.

Start by discussing any existing debts either of you may have. These could include student loans, credit card debts, car loans, or mortgages. Transparency about your debts is critical - it ensures both of you are aware of your total financial obligations.

Next, make a plan to tackle these debts. Prioritize high-interest debts, as these grow rapidly and can become burdensome. You might consider strategies like the 'debt snowball' method (paying off smaller debts first to gain momentum) or the 'debt avalanche' method (targeting the highest interest debts first to minimize interest payments).

Ensure your budget accounts for debt repayments, and automate these payments if possible. If your debts are significant and overwhelming, you might consider seeking advice from a credit counselor or financial advisor.

Incorporating Insurance

Insurance is a critical part of your financial foundation. It provides financial protection against significant risks, helping to ensure that an unexpected event doesn't derail your financial goals.

Discuss with your partner about the types of insurance that are most relevant for your situation. These might include health insurance, life insurance, home/renter's insurance, auto insurance, and disability insurance.

Review your current policies to ensure they provide adequate coverage, and consider where you may need additional insurance. Remember, the goal of insurance is not to prevent unexpected events but to protect against the financial impact of such events.

Creating an emergency fund, managing debt, and incorporating insurance into your financial plan are all integral steps in building a strong financial foundation. They equip you and your partner with the tools and resources to navigate financial uncertainties and set the stage for future financial growth. In the next part of this chapter, we will delve into long-term investment strategies and retirement planning, crucial components of your financial foundation.

Long-Term Investment Strategies

Once you've established an emergency fund, have a debt management plan in place, and have ensured adequate insurance, it's time to think about growing your wealth through investments.

Investing is not just for the wealthy; it's a financial strategy that can benefit everyone. It's about putting your money to work, so it grows over time, helping you achieve your long-term financial goals such as retirement, buying a house, or funding your children's education.

Before investing, it's crucial to understand that all investments involve some level of risk. However, by diversifying your investments and taking a long-term approach, you can mitigate these risks and increase the likelihood of generating a return.

Start by discussing with your partner about your risk tolerance, financial goals, and investment timelines. This conversation will guide your investment strategy. For example, if you're saving for retirement in 30 years, you can afford to take more risk and invest in growth-oriented assets like stocks. If you're saving for a down payment on a house in five years, you may want to stick to more conservative investments like bonds or high-yield savings accounts.

Consider working with a financial advisor or using robo-advisors to help you build a diversified portfolio. Regularly review and adjust your portfolio as your financial situation, goals, or market conditions change.

Retirement Planning

Planning for retirement is a crucial part of your financial foundation. The earlier you start, the more time your money has to grow, thanks to the power of compounding.

The first step in retirement planning is to have a conversation with your partner about what you envision for your retirement. When do you want to retire? What kind of lifestyle do you aspire to have? Do you plan to travel, pursue a hobby, or start a business?

Next, calculate how much you need to save for retirement. There are several online retirement calculators that can help you determine this number based on your age, income, desired retirement age, and projected expenses.

Consider maximizing your contributions to retirement accounts such as 401(k)s or Individual Retirement Accounts (IRAs). These accounts offer tax advantages that can help boost your retirement savings. If your employer offers a 401(k) match, try to contribute at least enough to get the full match—it's essentially free money towards your retirement.

The Role of Estate Planning

Estate planning, though often overlooked, is a crucial component of a comprehensive financial plan. It ensures that your assets are distributed according to your wishes after your death, and can also help reduce estate taxes and avoid probate.

At the very least, you and your partner should each have a will that outlines how you want your assets to be distributed. You should also designate beneficiaries for your retirement accounts and insurance policies.

If you have children, your estate plan should include provisions for their guardianship in case both of you pass away. If you have significant assets, you might also consider setting up a trust.

While it can be uncomfortable to think about death, having an estate plan can provide peace of mind that your loved ones will be taken care of and that your wishes will be honored.

In the next part of this chapter, we will discuss the role of continuous financial education in maintaining and enhancing your financial foundation, as well as how philanthropy can fit into your financial plan. Remember, building a strong financial foundation is a journey, not a destination. As your life circumstances change, your financial plan may need to be adjusted and updated. This is not a sign of failure, but a testament to the dynamic nature of financial planning.

Continuous Financial Education

A key pillar in the building and maintenance of your financial foundation is continuous financial education. The world of finance is dynamic, with evolving investment options, changing tax laws, and new financial products. Staying informed allows you to make better financial decisions and adapt your financial plan to changes in the financial landscape.

Set aside time to learn about personal finance together. Read books, listen to podcasts, follow finance blogs, or attend seminars or webinars. Topics could include investing, real estate, tax planning, retirement planning, or estate planning.

If you're comfortable doing so, consider sharing what you've learned with your children or other family members. Not only can this improve their financial literacy, but it can also foster deeper connections as you discuss financial goals, values, and strategies.

Philanthropy as Part of Your Financial Plan

For many couples, giving back to their communities or supporting causes they care about is an important part of their financial plan. Philanthropy can provide a sense of purpose and fulfillment, strengthen your connection as a couple, and even offer tax benefits.

Discuss with your partner about the causes or organizations you wish to support. You might choose to donate to a local charity, fund scholarships, support a global cause, or contribute to your alma mater.

You can incorporate philanthropy into your financial plan in several ways. You could allocate a certain percentage of your income to donations, include charitable organizations in your estate plan, or even create a donor-advised fund.

Remember, philanthropy isn't just about money; it can also involve volunteering your time or skills. The important thing is that you're making a positive difference in a way that aligns with your values and means.

Here is a list suggesting various philanthropy causes where a couple could allocate money:

Philanthropy Causes
Education
Healthcare
Environmental Conservation
Animal Welfare
Hunger Relief

Arts and Culture
Children and Youth
Social Justice
Women's Empowerment
Elderly Care
Disaster Relief
Community Development

This list provides a range of philanthropy causes to consider, but it is by no means an exhaustive list. Couples should have open and honest discussions to identify causes that resonate with their values and passions. Remember, philanthropy is a deeply personal choice, and it's important to choose causes that are meaningful to you and align with your shared values as a couple.

Putting It All Together

Building a strong financial foundation as a couple involves several elements, including an emergency fund, a debt management strategy, appropriate insurance, an investment plan, retirement planning, and estate planning. All of these elements need to work together to create a financial plan that supports your current needs and future goals.

As you work on each of these elements, you'll likely encounter challenges and disagreements. However, these challenges present opportunities for growth, both in your financial knowledge and your relationship. Remember, the goal isn't to create a perfect financial plan, but one that evolves and adapts with you as your life changes.

In the next chapter, "Money Mindset and Relationship Harmony," we'll explore the psychological aspects of managing money as a couple. We'll discuss how to cultivate a positive money mindset, how to navigate financial disagreements, and how to align your financial habits with your values for a harmonious and fulfilling relationship.

Building a strong financial foundation might seem complex, but remember that it's a journey you and your partner are embarking on together. As you take each step, you'll not only be building a secure financial future, but you'll also be strengthening your relationship. And in the end, isn't that what it's all about? So, embrace the journey, celebrate your progress, and keep moving forward, together.

4 MONEY MINDSET AND RELATIONSHIP HARMONY

As you continue on your financial journey together, it's essential to pay attention to not just the practical aspects of managing money but also the psychological aspects. Your beliefs, attitudes, and habits around money - what we refer to as your money mindset - can significantly impact your financial health and relationship harmony.

Understanding Your Money Mindset

Your money mindset is a set of beliefs and attitudes about money that you've developed over time, influenced by your upbringing, experiences, and societal messages. It shapes how you think about, feel, and behave around money.

There are many different money mindsets. You may have a scarcity mindset, characterized by the belief that there's never enough money, or an abundance mindset, where you believe there's always enough to go around. You might view money as a source of security, freedom, or power, or see it as a source of stress, conflict, or corruption.

It's crucial to identify and understand your money mindset because it can either help or hinder your financial and relationship goals. For example, if you equate money with security, you might be driven to save and invest, but also struggle with anxiety about losing money. If you view money as a source of power, you may strive to earn more, but also risk using money to control or manipulate.

Discussing Your Money Mindsets

To achieve financial harmony in your relationship, it's essential to understand not only your own money mindset but also your partner's. Start a conversation about your earliest memories of money, your beliefs about money, and how these beliefs influence your financial behaviors. You might discover, for example, that your partner's tendency to splurge on experiences stems from a belief that money should be used to create memories, not just accumulated.

Recognize that differences in money mindsets are natural and not necessarily bad. They reflect your unique experiences and perspectives and can bring balance to your financial decisions. For example, if one of you is more risk-averse and the other more risk-tolerant, you might end up with a balanced investment portfolio that aligns with your shared goals but isn't overly risky.

Cultivating a Shared Money Mindset

While honoring your individual money mindsets, it's beneficial to cultivate a shared money mindset that guides your financial decisions as a couple. This shared mindset should reflect your joint values, goals, and aspirations, and create a sense of unity and purpose in your financial journey.

Begin by discussing your shared values around money. Do you value financial security, generosity, financial independence, or something else? Next, discuss your shared financial goals and dreams. Do you aspire to retire early, travel the world, fund your children's education, start a business, or leave a legacy?

Then, combine these values and goals into a shared money mindset. For instance, "We believe in living within our means, investing in our future, and using our money to make a difference." This shared mindset can serve as a compass for your financial decisions, helping you stay aligned and focused on what matters most to you as a couple.

The Impact of Money Mindsets on Your Relationship

Your money mindsets can significantly impact your relationship, for better or for worse. If you view money similarly, it can lead to cohesion and harmony. But if you view money differently, it can lead to misunderstandings, disagreements, and conflict.

For example, if you view money as a source of security and your partner views it as a tool for enjoyment, you might clash over spending and saving decisions. You might feel anxious about your partner's spending, while your partner might feel stifled by your desire to save.

Understanding and respecting each other's money mindsets can help you navigate these conflicts. It allows you to see where your partner is coming from, express your own needs and fears, and find a middle ground that respects both of your perspectives.

In the next part of this chapter, we will delve into how to navigate financial disagreements, including how to communicate effectively about money, how to compromise, and how to repair after a financial disagreement. We will also explore how to align your financial habits with your shared money mindset and values, to create a harmonious and fulfilling financial life together.

Navigating Financial Disagreements

Even the most financially compatible couples experience disagreements over money. These disagreements can arise from differences in money mindsets, financial habits, or financial goals. However, the key to relationship harmony is not to avoid these disagreements but to navigate them in a way that strengthens your relationship and your financial partnership.

Communicating Effectively about Money

Effective communication is critical in navigating financial disagreements. It starts with creating a safe and respectful space to discuss money matters. Choose a time when both of you are calm and undistracted, and approach the conversation with an open mind and a willingness to understand each other's perspectives.

Use "I" statements to express your feelings, needs, and concerns. For example, instead of saying, "You're always wasting money on unnecessary things," say, "I feel anxious when I see our savings decreasing because I value financial security." This reduces defensiveness and promotes empathy.

Listen actively to your partner's perspective. Resist the urge to interrupt, defend, or solve the problem right away. Instead, try to understand your partner's feelings, needs, and concerns. Validate their perspective, even if you disagree with it.

Finding a Compromise

Once you understand each other's perspectives, work together to find a compromise that respects both of your needs and values. This might involve giving and taking on both sides.

For example, if one of you values saving for the future and the other values enjoying the present, you might agree to allocate a certain percentage of your income to savings, a certain percentage to discretionary spending, and a certain percentage to shared experiences. This allows both of you to meet your needs without undermining your joint financial goals.

Remember, compromise is not about winning or losing but about finding a solution that strengthens your financial partnership and your relationship. It requires flexibility, creativity, and a commitment to prioritize the relationship over individual preferences.

Repairing After a Financial Disagreement

Despite your best efforts, some financial disagreements might lead to hurt feelings, misunderstandings, or conflict. In these cases, it's essential to repair the damage to your relationship and your financial partnership.

Apologize if you've said or done something hurtful, and express appreciation for your partner's willingness to engage in the difficult conversation. Reaffirm your commitment to your shared financial goals and your relationship. Discuss what you can do differently next time to prevent or manage the disagreement better.

Remember, the goal of navigating financial disagreements is not just to resolve the disagreement but also to learn more about each other's money mindsets, strengthen your communication skills, and enhance your financial partnership.

Aligning Financial Habits with Your Shared Money Mindset and Values

Once you've established your shared money mindset and learned how to navigate financial disagreements, it's time to align your financial habits with your shared mindset and values.

If you value financial security, develop habits that support this value, such as saving a certain percentage of your income, minimizing unnecessary expenses, or investing wisely. If you value generosity, incorporate giving into your financial habits, whether by donating money, volunteering time, or supporting businesses that align with your values.

Developing aligned financial habits might involve breaking old habits and forming new ones. Be patient with yourself and each other during this process, and celebrate your progress along the way.

In the next part of this chapter, we'll discuss specific strategies for aligning your financial habits with your shared money mindset and values. We'll also explore how to maintain relationship harmony as you navigate financial changes and challenges together. As you continue on your financial journey, remember that your shared money mindset and your relationship harmony are just as important as your bank balance.

Strategies for Aligning Financial Habits with Your Shared Money Mindset

Your shared money mindset provides the compass for your financial decisions, but it's your day-to-day financial habits that propel you toward your financial goals. Here are some strategies to help align these habits with your shared money mindset and values:

1. **Budget Together**: One of the most effective ways to align your financial habits with your shared money mindset is to create a joint budget. This budget should reflect your shared financial goals, your individual needs and wants, and your shared values. Regularly review and update your budget to accommodate changes in your income, expenses, or goals.

2. **Establish Joint and Individual Accounts**: Having a joint account can help you manage shared expenses and save for shared goals. At the same time, maintaining individual accounts can allow for some financial independence and reduce disagreements over discretionary spending. Decide together how much of your income will go into each account.

3. **Automate Savings and Investments**: Make saving and investing a default habit by setting up automatic transfers to your savings or investment accounts. This not only ensures that you're consistently working towards your financial goals but also reduces the temptation to overspend.

4. **Set Spending Limits**: To prevent overspending and ensure you're living within your means, set spending limits for different categories, such as groceries, dining out, entertainment, and personal spending.

5. **Use Cash or Debit Cards for Discretionary Spending**: Using cash or debit cards for discretionary spending can help you stay aware of your spending and prevent credit card debt.

Maintaining Relationship Harmony Amid Financial Changes and Challenges

Life is filled with financial changes and challenges, from job loss and unexpected expenses to changes in income or financial goals. Navigating these changes together is not only essential for your financial health but also for maintaining relationship harmony.

1. **Communicate Regularly and Openly**: Regular financial check-ins can help you stay aligned on your financial goals, navigate financial changes, and preempt financial disagreements. During these check-ins, discuss your financial situation, progress towards goals, upcoming expenses, and any concerns or ideas you have.

2. **Be Flexible and Adaptable**: Your financial plan is not set in stone, but a living document that evolves with your life circumstances and goals. Be willing to adapt your plan as needed and be supportive of each other during financial transitions.

3. **Practice Empathy and Understanding**: Financial changes and challenges can bring up strong emotions, from fear and stress to disappointment or resentment. Be there for each other emotionally, provide a listening ear, offer words of reassurance, and remind each other of your shared values and goals.

4. **Stay Focused on Your Shared Goals**: Amid financial changes and challenges, keep your shared financial goals in sight. They will help you stay motivated, make tough financial decisions, and maintain a sense of partnership and purpose in your financial journey.

In the next part of this chapter, we'll delve deeper into the connection between financial behaviors and relationship satisfaction, exploring how working together towards financial goals can enhance relationship satisfaction, and how to balance financial responsibilities and power in a way that fosters equality and respect.

While money can be a source of stress and conflict in relationships, it can also be a tool for collaboration, mutual growth, and relationship enhancement. By understanding your money mindsets, navigating financial disagreements effectively, aligning your financial habits with your shared money mindset and values, and supporting each other through financial changes and challenges, you can achieve not just financial health but also relationship harmony.

**The Connection between Financial Behaviors and Relationship

Satisfaction**

Financial behaviors and relationship satisfaction are intertwined. While financial disagreements can lead to relationship dissatisfaction, working together towards financial goals can enhance relationship satisfaction.

Firstly, shared financial goals can give you a sense of purpose and direction, bringing you closer as a couple. Whether it's saving for a home, paying off debt, funding a dream vacation, or planning for retirement, these shared goals can turn managing money from a source of conflict into a collaborative project.

Moreover, financial success can enhance relationship satisfaction. Meeting financial goals not only improves your financial wellbeing but also boosts your confidence, reduces financial stress, and fosters a sense of accomplishment and unity in your relationship.

Lastly, managing money together can enhance your understanding and appreciation of each other. You get to see each other's strengths, resilience, creativity, and commitment in action. You learn to communicate, compromise, and support each other better. All of these can strengthen your bond and increase your satisfaction with your relationship.

Balancing Financial Responsibilities and Power

In a financially healthy and harmonious relationship, financial responsibilities and power are balanced. Both partners have an equal say in financial decisions, and both contribute to the financial wellbeing of the relationship, whether through earning, managing money, or supporting the partner's earning potential.

Balancing financial responsibilities starts with open communication. Discuss each other's strengths, interests, and schedules, and divide financial responsibilities accordingly. One partner might handle budgeting and bill payments, while the other handles investing and tax planning. Or, you might decide to handle all financial tasks together.

It's essential, however, that both partners are involved in financial decisions. This ensures that both partners' needs and perspectives are considered, and both have the knowledge and skills to manage money independently if needed.

Balancing financial power is equally important. Even if one partner earns more, both should have an equal say in how money is spent, saved, and invested. Both should also have access to money for their needs and wants.

To balance financial power, consider using a proportional or needs-based approach to handle joint expenses, and maintain some level of financial independence through individual accounts or personal spending allowances.

Conclusion

Your money mindset, financial behaviors, and relationship dynamics are intertwined. By understanding your individual and shared money mindsets, you can align your financial behaviors with your shared values and goals, navigate financial disagreements effectively, and balance financial responsibilities and power. These practices can not only improve your financial wellbeing but also enhance your relationship satisfaction.

In the next chapter, we'll delve into the connection between financial wellbeing and personal wellbeing. We'll discuss how financial stress affects your health and happiness, how to manage financial stress effectively, and how to use money to enhance your personal wellbeing. As you continue on your financial journey, remember that money is not an end in itself but a tool for creating a fulfilling life individually and as a couple.

Achieving financial harmony in your relationship is an ongoing journey of communication, understanding, collaboration, and growth. There will be challenges and disagreements, but with a shared money mindset, effective communication, and mutual respect, you can navigate these hurdles together and come out stronger as a couple. In the end, remember that the goal is not just financial health but also relationship harmony and personal wellbeing. Happy financial journey!

5 FINANCIAL PLANNING FOR A HARMONIOUS FUTURE

Financial success doesn't happen overnight. It's a process that requires planning, discipline, commitment, and patience. However, when couples undertake this journey together, it not only strengthens their financial stability but also strengthens their relationship, promoting a harmonious future.

The first part of financial planning involves setting clear, achievable financial goals. These should reflect both partners' dreams, needs, and values. Discuss what each of you wants to achieve financially in the short term (1-3 years), medium-term (4-10 years), and long term (10+ years). This could be anything from paying off debt to saving for a down payment for a house, funding your children's education, or planning for retirement.

It's vital that both partners have a say in setting these goals to ensure that they reflect shared values and priorities. It's also essential to make these goals specific, measurable, achievable, relevant, and time-bound (SMART). This makes the goals more motivating and allows you to track your progress effectively.

Creating a Financial Plan

Once you've set your financial goals, the next step is to create a financial plan to achieve these goals. This involves determining the amount you need to save or invest for each goal, the timeframe for achieving the goal, and the steps you need to take to reach the goal.

The financial plan should also include a budget that outlines your income, expenses, savings, and investments. This budget should be realistic, flexible, and aligned with your financial goals. It should also take into account occasional expenses and potential financial emergencies.

Remember, the financial plan is not set in stone, but a dynamic tool that you should review and update regularly as your financial situation, goals, or circumstances change.

The Role of Financial Discipline

Creating a financial plan is one thing, but sticking to it is another. This is where financial discipline comes in. Financial discipline involves making conscious, intentional financial decisions that align with your financial plan and goals, even when it's challenging.

For instance, it might involve resisting impulse purchases, prioritizing needs over wants, saving or investing a certain percentage of your income, and reducing or eliminating debt. It also involves regularly reviewing your financial plan and adjusting your financial behaviors as needed.

Financial discipline can be challenging, especially when faced with temptations, pressures, or financial setbacks. However, when practiced consistently, it can lead to financial success and personal growth. It can also promote trust, cooperation, and respect in your relationship.

In the next part of this chapter, we will delve into the strategies for building financial discipline, the role of financial education in financial planning, and the benefits of seeking professional financial advice. We will also discuss the importance of financial transparency in maintaining a harmonious relationship.

Achieving financial success as a couple is not just about the numbers but also about the journey. It's about learning to communicate effectively about money, understand each other's financial perspectives, make joint financial decisions, and support each other towards your financial goals. Through this journey, you can build not just financial wealth but also relationship wealth.

Building Financial Discipline

As we discussed in the previous section, financial discipline is a key ingredient of financial success. It involves making consistent, purposeful financial decisions that align with your financial plan and goals. Here are some strategies to help you build financial discipline:

1. **Automate Your Finances**: Automation can take the effort out of financial discipline. By setting up automatic transfers to your savings or investment accounts, or automatic payments for your bills, you can ensure that you're consistently working towards your financial goals and meeting your financial obligations.

2. **Use Tools and Apps**: Numerous tools and apps can help you track your spending, budgeting, saving, and investing. These tools can provide you

with insights into your financial behaviors, alert you to potential issues, and help you make informed financial decisions.

3. **Practice Delayed Gratification**: Delayed gratification involves resisting an immediate reward in favor of a larger or more enduring reward in the future. This can be a powerful strategy for building financial discipline, whether it's resisting an impulse purchase to save for a cherished goal or opting for a homemade meal instead of an expensive takeout to stay within your budget.

4. **Set Financial Boundaries**: Financial boundaries can help you avoid financial behaviors that undermine your financial goals or your relationship. These might include limits on discretionary spending, rules about discussing major financial decisions, or policies on lending or borrowing money.

The Role of Financial Education

Financial education plays a crucial role in financial planning. It equips you with the knowledge and skills to manage your money effectively, make informed financial decisions, and navigate financial challenges. It also empowers you to take control of your financial future and reduces your reliance on others for financial guidance.

Financial education can involve self-study, online courses, books, podcasts, or seminars on various financial topics, including budgeting, saving, investing, retirement planning, tax planning, and risk management. It can also involve learning about financial products, financial institutions, and financial regulations.

It's important to seek financial education from reliable, unbiased sources, and to continually update your financial knowledge to keep pace with the changing financial landscape.

The Benefits of Professional Financial Advice

While self-education is important, there may be times when you can benefit from professional financial advice. Financial advisors can provide personalized, comprehensive financial planning, including retirement planning, investment planning, tax planning, risk management, and estate planning. They can also provide guidance during financial transitions or challenges, such as job loss, inheritance, or market downturns.

When choosing a financial advisor, consider their qualifications, experience, services, fees, and approach to financial planning. Look for an advisor who is fiduciary, meaning they are obligated to act in your best interests.

The Importance of Financial Transparency

Financial transparency is crucial for financial harmony in a relationship. It involves being open about your financial situation, financial behaviors, financial decisions, and financial mistakes. It also involves discussing your financial expectations, concerns, and dreams with each other.

Financial transparency fosters trust, cooperation, and mutual understanding in your financial partnership. It also helps you make informed, inclusive financial decisions, avoid financial surprises or misunderstandings, and support each other towards your financial goals.

In the next part of this chapter, we will explore how to balance financial independence and financial cooperation in a relationship, how to adjust your financial plan for life's milestones and unexpected events, and how to instill financial values and habits in your children. We will also discuss the role of giving in financial planning.

Financial planning is a journey of growth, discovery, and partnership. It involves not just numbers, strategies, and plans, but also communication, understanding, discipline, education, transparency, and support. Through this journey, you can build a strong financial future and a stronger, happier relationship.

Balancing Financial Independence and Cooperation

A delicate balance exists in a relationship between maintaining financial independence and fostering financial cooperation. Both partners should have the autonomy to manage their finances and make financial decisions, but at the same time, cooperation is needed when it comes to shared financial goals and responsibilities.

There are various ways to strike this balance. Some couples opt for a joint account for shared expenses and individual accounts for personal expenses. Others choose to pool all their money together, while some prefer keeping finances completely separate.

What's important is to have a discussion about what system works best for your relationship and is in line with your shared financial goals. This balance can shift over time, and should be revisited regularly to ensure it is still serving your evolving needs and circumstances.

Planning for Life's Milestones and Unexpected Events

Life is full of unexpected events and milestones. Some are joyous, like having a baby or buying a new home, while others can be challenging, like job loss or a health crisis. Your financial plan should be flexible enough to adapt to these changes.

When planning for life's milestones, consider the financial implications and plan accordingly. For example, if you're planning to start a family, you might need to budget for pregnancy, childbirth, childcare, and education costs. If you're planning to buy a house, you might need to save for a down payment, closing costs, and home maintenance.

Planning for unexpected events, on the other hand, involves creating a financial safety net. This can include an emergency fund to cover three to six months' worth of living expenses, insurance to protect against major financial risks, and a diversified investment portfolio to weather market fluctuations.

Instilling Financial Values and Habits in Your Children

As parents, you have a unique opportunity to instill financial values and habits in your children. This can help them become financially responsible and savvy adults, and can also affect their relationship with money and their future partners.

To educate your children about money, involve them in financial activities, like shopping, budgeting, or saving. Share your financial values, goals, and mistakes, and discuss financial topics, like earning, spending, saving, investing, and giving. Teach them about the benefits of financial discipline, the dangers of debt, and the importance of financial planning.

You can also encourage financial independence by providing a small allowance or opportunities to earn money, and guiding them on how to manage this money effectively.

The Role of Giving in Financial Planning

Finally, consider the role of giving in your financial plan. Giving can take many forms, from donating money or items to volunteering time or skills. It can provide emotional rewards, foster a sense of purpose and community, and teach valuable lessons about empathy, generosity, and gratitude.

Incorporating giving into your financial plan can involve setting a giving budget, choosing causes or organizations that align with your values, and exploring various ways to give effectively. It can also involve teaching your children about giving and involving them in your giving activities.

In the next part of this chapter, we will explore the importance of celebrating financial victories, the role of gratitude in financial planning, and the connection between financial health and mental health. We will also reflect on the broader meaning of wealth and success.

Financial planning is more than a means to an end. It's a journey that shapes your character, your relationship, and your life. It's an opportunity to express your values, fulfill your dreams, navigate life's ups and downs, make a difference in the world, and leave a legacy for future generations.

Celebrating Financial Victories

Every financial goal you achieve, no matter how small, is a victory that deserves to be celebrated. This not only reinforces positive financial behaviors but also makes the financial journey more enjoyable and motivating.

Celebrating financial victories can involve a special meal, a small gift, a fun outing, or simply a heartfelt acknowledgment. However, be careful not to splurge in a way that undermines your financial goals. The celebration should be proportionate to the achievement and within your financial means.

The Role of Gratitude in Financial Planning

Gratitude plays a vital role in financial planning. It helps you appreciate what you have, reduces the desire for more, fosters contentment, and promotes financial peace.

To cultivate gratitude, consider practices like keeping a gratitude journal, expressing gratitude to each other, or meditating on gratitude. Also, when faced with financial challenges or sacrifices, try to find something positive or valuable in the situation.

The Connection between Financial Health and Mental Health

Financial health and mental health are closely connected. Financial stress can lead to anxiety, depression, sleep problems, relationship issues, and other mental health problems. Conversely, mental health problems can impair your ability to manage your finances and make sound financial decisions.

To safeguard your mental health, it's crucial to manage financial stress effectively. This can involve financial planning, financial education, seeking professional help, practicing self-care, and nurturing a positive, balanced attitude towards money.

Reflecting on the Broader Meaning of Wealth and Success

In the pursuit of financial goals, it's important to remember that wealth and success have a broader meaning. They encompass not just financial wealth, but also relationship wealth, emotional wealth, intellectual wealth, physical wealth, and spiritual wealth.

Similarly, success is not just about achieving financial goals or accumulating wealth. It's about leading a meaningful, fulfilling, and balanced life. It's about nurturing loving relationships, making a difference in the world, growing as a person, enjoying life's simple pleasures, and being true to yourself.

As you continue your financial journey, keep sight of this broader perspective. Let it guide your financial decisions, shape your financial goals, and define your measures of success. Let it inspire you to build not just a wealth of money, but a wealth of love, joy, wisdom, health, and spirit.

Here is a timeline of typical milestones in a couple's financial journey, from marriage to retirement:

Marriage: The beginning of the financial partnership. Couples establish joint bank accounts, discuss financial goals, and create a budget that aligns with their shared vision.

Building Emergency Fund: Establishing an emergency fund to cover unexpected expenses, typically 3-6 months' worth of living expenses, provides financial security.

Purchasing a Home: Saving for a down payment and buying a home requires careful financial planning. Couples consider mortgage options, evaluate affordability, and navigate the home buying process.

Starting a Family: Expanding the family brings new financial responsibilities. Couples plan for pregnancy and childbirth expenses, childcare costs, and budget for the child's future needs like education and healthcare.

Investing for the Future: Couples prioritize long-term financial goals such as retirement and begin investing in retirement accounts, stocks, bonds, or other investment vehicles to build wealth over time.

Paying Off Debt: Couples focus on paying off any outstanding debts, such as student loans, credit cards, or car loans, to reduce financial burdens and improve their financial standing.

Career Advancement: Both partners may experience career growth and increased income. Couples leverage this opportunity to boost savings, investments, and achieve financial milestones.

Maximizing Retirement Savings: As retirement approaches, couples contribute the maximum allowable amounts to retirement accounts, explore additional retirement savings options, and regularly review their retirement plans.

Empty Nesters: With children grown and independent, couples adjust their financial plan, considering downsizing, revisiting retirement goals, and reallocating resources to enjoy their post-parenting years.

Retirement: Couples reach the milestone of retirement, transitioning from a focus on saving to managing and enjoying their accumulated wealth. They establish a retirement income strategy and pursue activities that bring fulfillment and happiness.

Remember, this timeline serves as a general guide, and each couple's financial journey will vary based on their unique circumstances and aspirations. It's important to regularly assess and adjust your financial plan to stay on track and adapt to life's changes.

In Conclusion

Financial planning is a journey of love, growth, and partnership. It requires effort, patience, and persistence, but the rewards are well worth it.

Not only can it bring financial stability, freedom, and peace, but it can also bring a deeper understanding, a stronger bond, and a richer life.

Remember, every couple's financial journey is unique, influenced by their dreams, values, circumstances, and experiences. There is no one-size-fits-all approach to financial planning. What matters is to find the approach that fits you, respects both partners, and serves your shared dreams and values.

We hope this chapter has provided you with insights, tools, and inspiration to embark on your financial journey. In the next chapter, we will delve into the concept of financial infidelity, its impact on relationships, and ways to prevent and overcome it.

Remember, in this journey, you're not alone. You have each other. You have your love, your commitment, your dreams, your strengths, and your growth. You also have this book and the community of couples who are undertaking the same journey. Together, you can overcome financial challenges, achieve financial goals, and create a bright, harmonious financial future.

6 NAVIGATING FINANCIAL CHALLENGES TOGETHER

Life is unpredictable, and even the most meticulously laid financial plans can be disrupted by unforeseen circumstances. Job loss, medical emergencies, unexpected expenses, or a global financial crisis can all put severe strain on your finances. When these situations arise, it's easy to feel overwhelmed. However, facing these challenges head-on and together can reinforce your partnership and make your relationship stronger.

In the realm of economics, the only predictable constant is the periodic ebb and flow of financial crises. Just as the sun rises and sets, financial crises come and go periodically. It's essential for every couple to be prepared to navigate these challenging times. Reflecting on significant financial crises of the past, such as the oil crisis of the 1970s, the stock market crash of 1987, the dot-com bubble burst in the early 2000s, and the global financial crisis of 2008, we recognize the profound impact they had on the economy and individuals. These experiences have taught us the value of financial preparedness, risk management, and adaptability in the face of uncertainty. By embracing the lessons learned from these crises and implementing prudent financial practices, couples can strengthen their resilience, protect their financial well-being, and confidently navigate through any challenging times that may lie ahead.

This chapter aims to equip you with the tools, perspectives, and strategies needed to navigate financial challenges together, strengthening your bond and ensuring that your shared financial goals remain within reach.

Understanding Financial Stress

Financial stress is an inevitable part of dealing with financial challenges. It can lead to feelings of anxiety, depression, fear, and even anger. It's essential to recognize these emotions and understand that it's normal to feel this way when you're under financial pressure.

When experiencing financial stress, communication becomes even more critical. Discuss your fears and concerns openly with your partner. This isn't a time for blame but a time for coming together to find a way forward. Remember, you're a team, and every challenge is an opportunity to strengthen your relationship.

Building a Crisis Budget

In times of financial difficulty, one of the first steps to take is to reassess your budget. You'll need to differentiate between wants and needs, cutting back on non-essential expenses. This doesn't mean that you have to give up everything that brings you joy, but rather that you prioritize your spending to ensure the critical bills are paid first.

Building a crisis budget involves a clear-eyed assessment of your current spending habits. Begin by listing your income sources and all your expenses. Identify areas where you can make cuts, such as eating out less often, canceling unnecessary subscriptions, or postponing major purchases.

While this exercise can be difficult, it's important to approach it as a temporary measure to navigate through the crisis. Once your situation improves, you can gradually return to your regular budget, perhaps with a better appreciation for the distinction between wants and needs.

Consolidating and Paying Off Debt

Financial challenges often come with the burden of mounting debt. Whether it's credit card debt, a mortgage, or student loans, it's essential to create a strategy to manage and pay off this debt effectively.

Consider consolidating your debt, which could simplify your payments and potentially lower your interest rate. Explore different options for debt consolidation, such as a balance transfer credit card, a personal loan, or a home equity loan.

As for paying off your debt, two popular strategies are the "snowball method" (paying off smaller debts first to gain momentum) and the "avalanche method" (paying off debts with the highest interest rates first to minimize interest). Choose a strategy that best fits your circumstances and motivates you to keep going.

In the next part of this chapter, we will discuss how to deal with job loss, strategies for saving money during challenging times, and the importance of maintaining a positive mindset. We will also explore resources and tools that can help you navigate financial challenges more effectively.

Remember, challenges are a part of life, but they are also temporary. With resilience, flexibility, teamwork, and a sound strategy, you can navigate through any financial storm and come out stronger on the other side.

Coping with Job Loss

Job loss can be a significant financial challenge that leaves you with a sudden drop in income and uncertainty about the future. When faced with this situation, it's important to take a series of immediate steps to safeguard your finances.

Firstly, apply for any benefits you may be entitled to, such as unemployment benefits. Check your eligibility for other assistance programs like food and housing aid, and don't hesitate to use these resources during your time of need.

Next, revisit your crisis budget and adjust it according to your new income level. While you're job hunting, try to minimize expenses as much as possible without compromising your mental health and quality of life.

Don't forget to use this period as an opportunity for professional growth. Consider improving your skills, networking, and exploring other career avenues that may have been unavailable or unappealing in the past.

Saving Money in Difficult Times

Even in challenging financial times, the importance of saving cannot be overstated. While it might seem daunting or even impossible to save when you're barely making ends meet, every little bit counts.

Review your spending habits and identify areas where you can save money. This could be anything from reducing energy usage at home to preparing meals instead of eating out. Consider shopping second-hand or trading items with friends or family instead of buying new.

At the same time, look for ways to boost your income. This could involve selling items you no longer need, starting a side hustle, or freelancing. Remember, these are temporary measures to get through challenging times, but they can also serve as valuable life lessons in frugality and resourcefulness.

Maintaining a Positive Mindset

Staying positive during a financial crisis is undoubtedly a challenge, but it's crucial for your mental health and the overall wellbeing of your relationship. Understand that it's okay to feel stressed or anxious. However, try not to dwell on the negative and instead focus on the actions you can take to improve your situation.

Practice gratitude for what you have and celebrate small victories, whether it's sticking to your budget, paying off a debt, or securing a job interview. Lean on each other for emotional support and remind yourselves of your shared goals and dreams. You are more than your financial situation, and this challenging time does not define you or your relationship.

Utilizing Financial Tools and Resources

Numerous tools and resources are available to help you navigate financial challenges. These include budgeting apps, financial planning tools, debt calculators, online courses, and self-help books. Use these tools to track your spending, manage your debt, learn about finance, and stay motivated.

In the next part of this chapter, we will delve into the role of emergency funds, how to deal with medical emergencies and unexpected expenses, and how to rebuild your finances after a crisis. The journey might be tough, but remember, you're in it together, and together, you are stronger.

The Lifeline of Emergency Funds

An emergency fund is a cornerstone of financial stability, acting as a safety net during times of financial distress. Whether it's a job loss, medical emergency, or an unexpected repair, having an emergency fund can help you navigate these challenges without going into debt.

If you don't have an emergency fund, start building one as soon as you can. Aim to save enough to cover three to six months' worth of living expenses. Even if you can only save a small amount each month, it's a start. Remember, the goal is to build this fund gradually.

If you already have an emergency fund, be mindful about when to use it. It's intended for unexpected and necessary expenses, not discretionary or planned purchases. After you've used some of your emergency funds, focus on replenishing it when your financial situation stabilizes.

Dealing with Medical Emergencies and Unexpected Expenses

Medical emergencies and unexpected expenses can wreak havoc on your finances, especially if you're uninsured or underinsured. However, there are several ways to manage these costs.

Firstly, discuss payment options with your healthcare provider. They may offer payment plans that allow you to pay the bill over time. Additionally, some hospitals and medical providers have charity care programs, sliding-scale fees, or other forms of financial assistance.

For other unexpected expenses, such as a major car repair or home repair, consider if it's an immediate necessity or if it can be postponed. If it's an immediate need, look for ways to reduce the cost. This could mean shopping around for cheaper services, doing some tasks yourself, or buying used parts or equipment.

Prioritizing Mental Health

Financial challenges can take a heavy toll on mental health, leading to stress, anxiety, and depression. Therefore, prioritizing mental health is crucial during these challenging times.

First, recognize the signs of financial stress, such as constant worry about money, difficulty sleeping, or conflicts with your partner about finances. Don't ignore these signs or dismiss them as just "part of life." Acknowledge your feelings and seek support if needed.

Practices such as meditation, exercise, hobbies, and connecting with loved ones can help alleviate stress and promote mental wellbeing. Consider seeking professional help if financial stress becomes overwhelming or leads to persistent feelings of sadness or anxiety.

In the final part of this chapter, we will discuss how to rebuild your finances after a crisis, the importance of financial forgiveness, and the role of financial planning in preventing future financial crises. The journey through financial challenges can be tough, but with resilience, perseverance, and teamwork, you can overcome these hurdles and emerge stronger.

Rebuilding Finances After a Crisis

Recovering financially after a crisis is a gradual process, and it's essential to approach it with patience and realistic expectations.

Start by reassessing your financial situation and defining your new financial goals. These may be different from your previous goals, considering the changes brought about by the crisis. This could involve rebuilding your emergency fund, paying off debt accumulated during the crisis, or saving for a major upcoming expense.

Next, revise your budget according to your current income, expenses, and financial goals. Allocate funds towards your most immediate needs first, such as housing, food, utilities, and essential healthcare. Then, assign money towards your financial goals. If your income doesn't cover your expenses and financial goals, look for ways to reduce costs or increase income.

Lastly, consider seeking professional help. A financial adviser can provide guidance on managing debt, rebuilding savings, investing wisely, and planning for the future. They can also provide reassurance and help you navigate complex financial decisions.

After a crisis, there are often numerous good investment opportunities that arise. While it's crucial to approach investments with caution and thorough research, the aftermath of a crisis can present favorable conditions for long-term growth and financial gains.

As the economy recovers, sectors and industries that were heavily impacted may offer attractive prospects for investors. However, it's essential to carefully assess the risks and potential returns associated with each opportunity.

Consider diversifying your investments to mitigate risk and consult with a financial advisor who can provide valuable insights and help identify promising investment avenues. With a strategic approach and proper guidance, couples can take advantage of post-crisis opportunities to rebuild and strengthen their financial position for the future.

The Importance of Financial Forgiveness

Financial mistakes are an inevitable part of life, and during a crisis, the likelihood of making such mistakes can increase. In these moments, it becomes paramount for couples to embrace the concept of financial forgiveness. Rather than harboring blame and resentment, financial forgiveness allows couples to navigate through difficult times with empathy, understanding, and a focus on growth.

Understanding the Reasons

When financial mistakes occur, it's important to take a step back and understand the reasons behind them. Rather than jumping to conclusions or assigning blame, approach the situation with an open mind and a willingness to empathize. Recognize that financial decisions are often influenced by various factors, such as stress, fear, or a lack of information. By understanding the underlying reasons, you can foster a more compassionate and supportive environment.

Learning from Mistakes

Every financial mistake provides an opportunity for growth and learning. Instead of dwelling on the past, shift your focus towards the lessons that can be derived from the experience. Reflect on what went wrong and discuss with your partner how to prevent similar mistakes in the future. By treating mistakes as valuable learning opportunities, you can develop stronger financial habits and enhance your decision-making skills as a couple.

Open Communication and Transparency

Financial forgiveness requires open communication and transparency between partners. It's crucial to create a safe space where both individuals feel comfortable discussing their financial missteps without fear of judgment or retaliation. Establish a habit of regular check-ins to review your financial progress, share concerns, and address any mistakes or challenges that arise. By fostering an environment of open communication, you can build trust and strengthen your financial partnership.

Letting Go of Blame and Guilt

Financial forgiveness is about releasing blame, guilt, and negative emotions associated with past mistakes. Holding onto these negative feelings can strain your relationship and impede your financial recovery. Instead, focus on the present and future, acknowledging that mistakes are a natural part of the learning process. By letting go of blame and guilt, you create space for healing, growth, and the opportunity to make better financial decisions together.

Supporting Each Other

In times of financial mistakes, it's crucial to remember that you and your partner are a team. Teams support and uplift each other, even in moments of failure. By offering support, encouragement, and understanding, you create an environment where forgiveness can flourish. Show empathy towards your partner's financial struggles, be patient with each other, and work together to overcome challenges. Embrace the mindset that, as a couple, you are in this together, and together, you can overcome any financial obstacle.

Moving Forward and Growing Together

Financial forgiveness is an essential element of nurturing a healthy and resilient relationship. It allows couples to move forward, not forgetting the mistakes but releasing the negative emotions attached to them. Through understanding, learning, open communication, and mutual support, you can grow together as a couple. Embrace the opportunities for growth that financial mistakes present, strengthen your financial partnership, and create a future founded on trust, forgiveness, and shared financial goals.

Preventing Future Financial Crises

While you can't prevent all financial crises, financial planning can help you be better prepared for them. An emergency fund, adequate insurance, diversified investments, and a flexible budget can all contribute to financial resilience.

Moreover, regular financial check-ins and open communication about finances can help you detect potential financial problems early and address them proactively. Financial education can also empower you to make sound financial decisions and navigate financial challenges effectively.

In conclusion, navigating financial challenges as a couple can be tough, but it can also be an opportunity for growth, resilience, and deeper connection. The strategies and perspectives discussed in this chapter can help you turn financial challenges from relationship hurdles into relationship strengtheners. Remember, the key is to face the challenges together, support each other, stay open to learning, and never lose sight of your shared dreams and values.

In the next chapter, we'll explore how to foster financial harmony in your relationship, ensuring that money becomes a tool for nurturing love, happiness, and fulfillment. Stay tuned and remember, together, you are stronger.

7 LOVE AND MONEY: BALANCING ROMANCE AND FINANCES

Money, often cited as a leading cause of stress in relationships, can also be a tool for nurturing love, understanding, and mutual respect. The intersection of love and money isn't always straightforward, but it provides an opportunity to build a stronger bond based on shared values and goals.

In this chapter, we'll delve into the nuances of balancing romance and finances. We'll provide insights into maintaining intimacy and romance while being responsible with your money, demonstrating that love isn't about lavish gifts or extravagant dates, but meaningful moments, understanding, and shared experiences.

Money Conversations and Relationship Health

Open and honest communication about finances forms the bedrock of a financially healthy relationship. Such conversations aren't always easy and may sometimes lead to disagreements, but they are necessary. They not only facilitate practical financial management but also foster trust and deepen understanding.

To make money talks productive, establish a no-blame environment. The aim isn't to criticize each other's spending habits but to understand your respective financial attitudes, find common ground, and develop shared financial goals.

Ensure that these conversations are ongoing. Regular financial check-ins can help you stay on track with your goals, adapt to changes in your financial situation, and mitigate potential financial issues before they escalate.

The Role of Financial Compatibility

Financial compatibility doesn't mean that you and your partner need to have identical views about money. Rather, it means understanding each other's financial attitudes, respecting them, and finding ways to merge your financial lives without causing conflict or resentment.

If you and your partner have different spending habits or attitudes towards saving and investing, it's not a cause for alarm. These differences can lead to fruitful discussions, provide new perspectives, and even bring balance to your financial management.

If disagreements arise, try to find a compromise. For instance, if one of you is a spender and the other a saver, agree on a budget that allows for discretionary spending but also contributes to savings. If one of you is risk-averse and the other a risk-taker when it comes to investments, construct a diversified investment portfolio that caters to both your risk appetites.

In the next parts of this chapter, we'll explore practical ways of maintaining romance while managing finances responsibly, provide ideas for affordable yet meaningful dates, and discuss thoughtful gestures that don't require you to break the bank. The goal is to help you understand that love and money can coexist harmoniously, with money being a tool to express love and build a shared future, rather than a source of conflict and stress.

The Art of Frugal Romance

In today's society, we often associate romance with grand gestures and expensive gifts. However, true romance lies in the emotional connection, shared experiences, and understanding between partners, not the price tag of your expressions of love.

This segment emphasizes the art of frugal romance, allowing you to maintain the flame of love without straining your financial goals.

Meaningful yet Inexpensive Dates

Creating romantic experiences does not necessitate spending a fortune. With a bit of creativity, you can plan meaningful and fun dates on a budget. Here are ten ideas to inspire your next affordable and memorable outing:

1. **Nature Dates:** Explore the beauty of the outdoors by planning a picnic in a local park, going for a scenic hike, visiting a nearby beach, or simply stargazing in your backyard. These activities not only provide breathtaking settings but also offer opportunities to connect away from the distractions of everyday life.

2. **At-Home Movie Night:** Transform your living room into a cozy

cinema by choosing a favorite movie or series, preparing some popcorn, and creating your own movie experience at home. Snuggling up together under a blanket while enjoying a film is a simple yet romantic way to spend quality time together.

3. **DIY Project:** Engage in a do-it-yourself project together. It could be a home renovation task, gardening, crafting, or even painting. Not only will you be creating something together, but you'll also learn new skills, discover hidden talents, and deepen your bond as you work side by side.

4. **Cooking Together:** Plan a cooking night where you both take charge of preparing a delicious meal. Choose a recipe you've been eager to try, gather the necessary ingredients, and embark on a culinary adventure. Not only will you save money by dining at home, but you'll also have a delightful time collaborating in the kitchen and savoring the fruits of your labor.

5. **Bookstore or Library Date:** Spend an afternoon exploring a local bookstore or library together. Browse through the aisles, pick out books that intrigue you, and share your favorite finds with each other. It's a fantastic way to indulge in your shared love for reading while engaging in meaningful conversations.

6. **Artistic Endeavors:** Tap into your creativity by visiting an art gallery or attending a local art exhibition. Admire the works of talented artists, discuss your interpretations, and perhaps even be inspired to create your own art afterward. Expressing yourselves artistically can be a unique and thought-provoking experience.

7. **Volunteer Together:** Dedicate a few hours to a shared cause by volunteering at a local charity or community organization. Working together to help others not only strengthens your bond but also allows you to make a positive impact on the lives of those in need.

8. **Outdoor Sports or Games:** Enjoy some friendly competition and physical activity by engaging in outdoor sports or games. Play a game of tennis, go for a bike ride, challenge each other to a round of mini-golf, or have a playful picnic with frisbee or catch. These activities promote teamwork, laughter, and a healthy dose of fun.

9. **Cultural Exploration:** Take advantage of free or low-cost cultural events in your area, such as art exhibitions, music concerts, dance performances, or local festivals. Immerse yourselves in different forms of art and culture, embracing the diversity of experiences that your community has

to offer.

10. **Scenic Drives or Bike Rides:** Embark on a scenic drive or bike ride together to explore the beauty of your surroundings. Discover hidden gems, enjoy picturesque landscapes, and create lasting memories as you venture into new territories.

Remember, the true essence of a date lies in the quality time and connection you share with your partner. By embracing these inexpensive yet meaningful date ideas, you can cultivate a deeper bond, create cherished memories, and strengthen your relationship without breaking the bank.

Thoughtful Gestures over Expensive Gifts

Expensive gifts can be a nice treat, but they are not the cornerstone of expressing love. Thoughtful gestures, no matter how small, often hold more emotional value. Here are ten ideas for meaningful gestures that can strengthen your connection:

1. **Handwritten Letters:** In the digital age, a handwritten letter stands out as a deeply personal and thoughtful gesture. It shows that you've taken the time to pen your thoughts and feelings, creating a tangible keepsake that your partner can cherish.

2. **Doing Chores for Them:** Taking over your partner's chores when they're stressed or tired is a practical way of saying "I care about you." It lightens their load and provides them with some well-deserved relaxation or leisure time.

3. **Remembering Small Details:** Paying attention to your partner's likes, dislikes, and preferences and incorporating these into your actions shows that you listen and value their individuality. Surprise them with their favorite snack, plan an outing to their preferred spot, or gift them something that aligns with their hobbies or interests.

4. **Spending Quality Time:** Undivided attention is one of the most valued gifts you can give your partner. Designate specific times when you put away distractions and focus entirely on each other. Engage in meaningful conversations, go for walks, or simply cuddle up and enjoy each other's company.

5. **Acts of Service:** Offering to help with tasks or responsibilities that

your partner finds challenging or overwhelming demonstrates your support and care. Whether it's running errands, preparing a meal, or assisting with a project, these acts of service alleviate their burden and show that you're in their corner.

6. **Surprise Notes or Texts:** Leave little surprise notes or send thoughtful texts throughout the day to let your partner know you're thinking of them. These small gestures can brighten their day and remind them of your love and appreciation.

7. **Cooking Their Favorite Meal:** Prepare a special meal tailored to your partner's tastes. Cooking their favorite dish or surprising them with a homemade treat can create a delightful and intimate experience that shows you've put effort and thought into nourishing their body and soul.

8. **Supporting Their Goals:** Show genuine interest in your partner's aspirations and actively support their endeavors. Encourage their dreams, offer assistance when needed, and celebrate their achievements. Your unwavering support can be a powerful source of motivation and inspiration.

9. **Plan Surprise Outings:** Organize surprise outings or activities that align with your partner's interests or desires. It could be a spontaneous picnic in the park, a day trip to a nearby town, or tickets to a show or event they've been wanting to attend. These unexpected experiences create lasting memories and demonstrate your thoughtfulness.

10. **Acts of Affection:** Simple gestures of affection can have a profound impact on your connection. Hugs, kisses, cuddling, holding hands, or expressing verbal affirmations of love and appreciation all contribute to a loving and nurturing relationship.

Remember, it's the thought and effort behind these gestures that make them truly meaningful. By incorporating these thoughtful acts into your daily lives, you can strengthen your bond, foster deeper intimacy, and create a love-filled partnership.

In the following segments, we will explore the concept of financial gestures of love, discuss how to manage financial disagreements in a healthy way, and touch on long-term financial planning as a couple. Remember, love is about the connection between two souls, and while money can facilitate expressions of love, it is not the measurement of love. The most precious gift you can offer in a relationship is your time, your understanding, and your authentic self.

Financial Gestures of Love

Financial gestures of love are acts that display care and understanding for your partner's financial well-being. These gestures can strengthen your relationship and signify a shared commitment to financial health. Here are ten meaningful financial gestures that can enhance your connection:

1. **Saving Together for a Common Goal:** Establishing a joint savings plan for a shared goal, such as a dream vacation, a home, or an emergency fund, demonstrates your commitment to a prosperous future together. It shows that you are actively working towards your shared dreams and aspirations.

2. **Taking Care of Shared Expenses:** Sharing the responsibility of managing shared expenses, such as bills and household costs, is a gesture of responsibility and consideration. It involves contributing to these expenses based on your individual capacities, ensuring a fair distribution and avoiding placing an undue financial burden on one partner.

3. **Investing in Each Other:** Demonstrating support for your partner's personal and professional growth by investing in their education, career development, or business venture is a powerful gesture of love. It conveys your belief in their potential and your commitment to their long-term success.

4. **Creating a Financial Safety Net:** Building an emergency fund together signifies your commitment to each other's financial security. It shows that you prioritize being prepared for unexpected expenses or challenging times, providing peace of mind and a sense of stability in your relationship.

5. **Budgeting Together:** Collaboratively creating and maintaining a budget fosters financial transparency and shared decision-making. It allows you to align your financial priorities, track your spending, and work together towards common financial goals.

6. **Celebrating Financial Milestones:** Recognizing and celebrating significant financial milestones, such as paying off debt, achieving savings targets, or reaching investment milestones, is an opportunity to acknowledge and appreciate each other's financial accomplishments. It encourages further progress and motivates both partners to continue working towards financial success.

7. **Supporting Financial Education:** Encouraging and supporting each other's financial education and literacy is a valuable gesture. This could involve sharing articles, attending financial workshops together, or discussing personal finance books. By investing in your financial knowledge collectively, you empower yourselves to make informed and wise financial decisions.

8. **Being Mindful of Each Other's Financial Priorities:** Showing sensitivity and respect for your partner's financial priorities, even if they differ from your own, is an act of love. It involves open and non-judgmental communication, acknowledging and understanding each other's values and aspirations, and finding compromises that honor both perspectives.

9. **Regular Financial Check-Ins:** Scheduling regular financial check-ins allows you to review your progress, address any concerns or challenges, and make adjustments to your financial plans together. It demonstrates your commitment to open communication and shared financial responsibility.

10. **Celebrating Financial Independence:** Celebrating each other's financial independence and achievements is crucial. Encouraging personal financial growth and recognizing each other's financial autonomy fosters a sense of empowerment and strengthens the bond of trust within your relationship.

Remember, financial gestures of love are not solely about money but about demonstrating care, support, and understanding for each other's financial well-being. By embracing these gestures, you can cultivate a deeper connection and build a strong foundation for a thriving and harmonious financial partnership.

Managing Financial Disagreements Healthily

Financial disagreements are common in relationships, but how you handle them determines their impact on your relationship and finances. Here are ten guidelines to help you navigate these disagreements in a healthy and productive way:

1. **Listen to Understand:** Practice active listening and seek to understand your partner's perspective. Give them the space to express their thoughts and feelings without interruption, allowing for a deeper understanding of their point of view.

2. **Communicate Calmly and Respectfully:** Keep discussions focused on the issue at hand and avoid resorting to blame, criticism, or contemptuous

language. Speak from a place of empathy and use "I" statements to express how you feel, fostering an environment of open and respectful communication.

3. **Find Common Ground:** Look for areas of agreement or shared goals amidst your differences. Identify the underlying interests and values behind your financial positions, and seek a compromise that honors both perspectives.

4. **Practice Financial Transparency:** Be open and honest about your financial situation, including income, expenses, debts, and financial goals. Transparency builds trust and helps create a solid foundation for discussing and resolving financial disagreements.

5. **Establish Boundaries:** Discuss and set clear boundaries regarding financial decision-making. Determine which financial decisions require joint approval and which ones can be made individually, respecting each other's autonomy while still maintaining a sense of shared financial responsibility.

6. **Prioritize Financial Goals:** Identify and prioritize your financial goals as a couple. By aligning your goals, you can work together towards a shared vision and make informed financial decisions that support your aspirations.

7. **Take Time-Outs if Needed:** If a discussion becomes heated or emotionally charged, it's important to recognize when a break is needed. Take a step back, breathe, and regroup later to resume the conversation with a clearer and calmer mindset.

8. **Seek Support from Professionals:** If financial disagreements persist or become overwhelming, consider seeking guidance from professionals such as financial advisors or relationship counselors. They can provide objective insights, strategies, and tools to help you navigate financial challenges as a couple.

9. **Practice Financial Compromise:** Recognize that compromise is an essential part of managing financial disagreements. It may require finding middle ground, exploring alternative solutions, or making trade-offs to find a resolution that satisfies both partners.

10. **Celebrate Progress and Learn from Mistakes:** Acknowledge and celebrate the progress you make in managing financial disagreements. Reflect on past disagreements as learning experiences, and use them to strengthen your communication skills and deepen your understanding of each other's

financial perspectives.

In the upcoming segments, we will delve into long-term financial planning as a couple and how to maintain individual financial identities while being part of a financial duo. Remember, balancing love and money isn't about putting a price tag on your relationship; it's about using money as a tool to enhance your relationship and build a future that reflects your shared dreams and values. By practicing healthy communication, mutual respect, and a willingness to compromise, you can navigate financial disagreements with grace and strengthen the bond between you and your partner.

Long-Term Financial Planning as a Couple

Long-term financial planning as a couple encompasses much more than merely paying bills together. It's about setting shared financial goals and charting a path towards those goals that align with your values and dreams as a couple.

1. **Set Shared Financial Goals:** Discuss your dreams and aspirations, then translate them into financial goals. Whether it's buying a home, starting a family, traveling the world, or retiring early, having shared financial goals gives your financial decisions a shared purpose.

2. **Develop a Financial Plan:** Once you have your goals, map out a plan to achieve them. This might involve budgeting, saving, investing, or reducing debt. Make sure the plan is realistic, flexible, and considers both partners' income, financial obligations, and personal preferences.

3. **Review and Adjust Regularly:** Your financial goals and plan aren't set in stone. Regularly review your progress and adjust your plan as necessary. Life changes, like a new job, a baby, or an illness, might require you to update your financial goals and strategies.

Maintaining Individual Financial Identities

While managing finances as a couple is important, it's equally crucial to maintain individual financial identities.

1. **Personal Spending Money:** Consider allocating a portion of your budget for each partner to spend as they wish. This gives you the freedom to make some financial decisions independently, which can help prevent resentment and maintain financial autonomy.

2. **Separate Accounts:** Having some separate finances can provide financial security and independence. You might choose to have individual accounts for personal expenses and a joint account for shared expenses.

3. **Individual Credit:** Maintaining individual credit histories and scores can provide financial protection in the event of divorce, the death of a partner, or if one partner has poor credit.

Balancing love and money is a delicate task that requires open communication, mutual respect, and shared decision-making. Remember, your aim should not just be to 'manage' money as a couple but to use it as a tool to build a happier, stronger, and more fulfilling relationship. In the last part of this chapter, we'll discuss the significance of celebrating financial victories together and how to nurture financial gratitude in your relationship. We hope that these insights help you perceive money not as a potential source of conflict but as a tool for nurturing love, intimacy, and mutual growth.

Celebrating Financial Victories Together

Celebrating financial victories, big or small, brings a sense of shared achievement and reinforces the spirit of teamwork in your financial journey.

1. **Recognize Progress:** Paying off debt, saving a certain amount, or sticking to your budget for a month might not seem like a big deal, but they are significant steps towards financial stability and independence. Acknowledge these achievements and appreciate each other's efforts.

2. **Celebrate Milestones:** When you achieve a financial goal, celebrate! It could be as simple as a special home-cooked meal or a night out. Celebrations not only add fun to your financial journey but also reinforce your commitment to your shared financial goals.

3. **Keep the Momentum Going:** After a victory, set your next goal and work towards it. This keeps the momentum going and maintains your focus on your long-term financial dreams.

Nurturing Financial Gratitude in Your Relationship

In your financial journey as a couple, it's easy to get caught up in what you don't have or what you aspire to achieve. However, cultivating gratitude for what you already have is vital.

1. **Acknowledge Your Partner's Contributions:** Regularly express appreciation for your partner's financial and non-financial contributions. This can enhance mutual respect and foster a positive relationship dynamic.

2. **Appreciate Your Achievements:** Make it a habit to reflect on your financial progress and express gratitude for what you've achieved. This helps you stay motivated and focused on your financial goals.

3. **Express Gratitude for the Little Things:** Simple gestures like preparing a meal, taking care of a bill, or working overtime to save for a common goal often go unnoticed. Yet, they reflect your partner's care and commitment. Acknowledge these acts and express your appreciation.

Balancing love and finances is a journey filled with learning, growth, and shared experiences. With open communication, shared financial goals, and a strong sense of mutual respect, you can navigate financial waters without straining your relationship. And always remember, in the grand scheme of love and life, money is just a tool. It's how you use that tool that determines the richness of your relationship and the quality of your shared life.

8 BLENDING FAMILIES AND FINANCES

Blending families - merging two families into one due to remarriage - is an act of love and commitment. However, it also brings unique financial challenges that need understanding, acceptance, and well-crafted strategies to navigate.

1. **Merging Different Financial Philosophies:** Different families often have varied financial practices and attitudes. These differences can cause confusion and discord when not addressed and harmonized properly.

2. **Supporting Children from Previous Relationships:** Providing for children from previous marriages or relationships while ensuring that all children feel equally loved and cared for can be a delicate balancing act.

3. **Dealing with Alimony or Child Support:** These ongoing expenses can significantly impact a family's financial landscape and need to be factored into the new family's financial plans.

4. **Inheritance Considerations:** Ensuring fair treatment of all children in terms of inheritance can be tricky, especially when considering biological and step-children.

Understanding these challenges is the first step in creating a cohesive financial plan that meets everyone's needs. It's crucial to approach these challenges with openness, respect, and a willingness to find common ground.

Building Open Communication Channels

Transparent communication is the cornerstone of successful financial management in blended families. It's necessary to discuss and understand each other's financial situations, obligations, and expectations to foster an atmosphere of trust and mutual respect.

1. **Discuss Finances Openly:** Both partners should be upfront about their financial obligations, including debts, alimony, child support, and other financial responsibilities related to their previous relationships.

2. **Talk about Financial Expectations:** Discuss your financial expectations, including how expenses for children will be handled, how

household costs will be divided, and how savings and investments will be managed.

3. **Involve Children When Appropriate:** Depending on their age and maturity level, involve children in financial discussions. This can help them understand the family's financial situation and teach them valuable lessons about money.

4. **Regular Financial Check-ins:** Regular family financial meetings can help keep everyone informed, provide a platform for discussing financial issues, and facilitate joint decision-making.

In the upcoming parts, we will discuss strategies for merging finances, managing expenses for children from previous relationships, creating a cohesive financial plan, and dealing with legal considerations for blended families. Remember, financial integration in blended families is a gradual process that requires patience, understanding, and plenty of communication. It's not just about making the numbers work; it's about creating a shared financial identity that respects everyone's needs and contributions.

Merging Finances: Finding the Middle Ground

Merging finances in a blended family is a complex task. It requires careful thought and delicate handling to ensure that it's fair and considerate of everyone's feelings and financial circumstances.

1. **Joint or Separate?:** Deciding whether to combine all finances, keep them entirely separate, or adopt a hybrid model is a personal choice. A joint account can be helpful for shared household expenses, but individual accounts may also be necessary to meet separate obligations or ensure personal financial autonomy.

2. **Equal or Proportional Contributions?:** Should each partner contribute equally to joint expenses, or should contributions be proportional to income? Both methods have their pros and cons, and the decision should be based on what feels fairest to both parties and the overall family dynamics.

3. **Managing Debts and Assets:** How should debts and assets brought into the marriage be handled? Clear agreements should be established regarding responsibility for pre-existing debts and ownership of personal assets.

4. **New Financial Commitments:** All new financial obligations - mortgages, car loans, credit cards - should be discussed in detail before any commitments are made. Both parties should agree on how these obligations will be met and how they might impact the family's overall financial health.

Managing Expenses for Children from Previous Relationships

Providing for children from previous relationships is often one of the most sensitive issues in a blended family.

1. **Clarity about Financial Responsibilities:** Be clear about who is responsible for which aspects of the children's expenses. This might be determined by legal agreements or mutual decisions within the family.

2. **Fairness, Not Equality:** Strive for fairness, not necessarily equality. For example, older children may have different financial needs than younger ones, such as college tuition or car insurance.

3. **Open Dialogue with Ex-Partners:** If applicable, maintain open communication with your ex-partner about shared financial responsibilities for your children. This can help avoid misunderstandings and ensure that your children's needs are adequately met.

Blending families and finances is a complex, nuanced journey, but with open communication, mutual respect, and shared decision-making, it's entirely possible to create a balanced financial life that supports each family member's needs. In the following sections, we will explore creating a unified financial plan and tackling the legal financial considerations unique to blended families. Your financial decisions should always aim at supporting the emotional health and happiness of your blended family, fostering an atmosphere of love, acceptance, and mutual respect.

Creating a Unified Financial Plan

As you merge your families and finances, it becomes essential to create a unified financial plan. This plan should reflect your combined financial goals, resources, obligations, and aspirations for the future.

1. **Shared Financial Goals:** Discuss and agree on shared financial goals. These might include saving for a larger home to accommodate your blended family, funding higher education for the children, or planning for retirement.

Shared goals can foster a sense of teamwork and shared purpose.

2. **Budgeting for a Blended Family:** Designing a budget for a blended family can be more complex than for a traditional family. It should account for child support or alimony payments, expenses related to children from previous relationships, and any costs related to maintaining relationships with ex-spouses, like travel.

3. **Saving and Investing:** Agree on strategies for saving and investing. This should take into account the risk tolerance and financial goals of each partner, as well as the need to secure the financial future of all children.

4. **Insurance and Emergency Planning:** It's crucial to plan for unexpected events. You might need to adjust life insurance policies, update beneficiaries, and ensure that you have an emergency fund that can support your blended family.

Addressing the Legal Aspects

Blended families often need to navigate several legal aspects related to finances, particularly concerning child support, alimony, and inheritance.

1. **Child Support and Alimony:** Be aware of the legal implications of your child support and alimony obligations. Ensure that your budget accurately reflects these obligations, and remember that failing to meet them can have severe legal consequences.

2. **Estate Planning:** Blended families often face more complex estate planning challenges. Wills and other estate planning documents should be updated to reflect the new family structure, with careful consideration given to the needs of all children and partners.

3. **Prenuptial Agreements:** While not romantic, prenuptial agreements can be particularly beneficial in blended families. These agreements can specify what will happen to assets in the event of a divorce, providing clarity and protecting all parties.

As you navigate the financial journey of a blended family, remember that there are no one-size-fits-all solutions. Each family is unique and deserves a financial plan that respects and meets its distinct needs. In the final part of this chapter, we'll explore strategies for nurturing a positive money mindset in your blended family and practical tips for making the financial blending process smoother. Let's remember: this journey is not merely about money; it's about fostering a loving, respectful, and inclusive family environment where everyone feels secure and valued.

Nurturing a Positive Money Mindset in Your Blended Family

A positive money mindset can significantly influence your family's financial behaviors and outcomes. Here's how you can nurture this within your blended family:

1. **Practice Openness and Honesty:** Encourage openness about money-related matters. Transparent conversations can reduce misunderstandings and create a sense of trust.

2. **Teach Money Management Skills:** Foster financial literacy among your children. Teach them budgeting, saving, and wise spending habits to set them up for financial success.

3. **Model Positive Financial Behaviors:** Your actions speak louder than your words. Display responsible financial behaviors that your children can emulate.

4. **Avoid Money Taboos:** Do not allow money to become a taboo topic. Encourage curiosity and answer money-related questions to the best of your ability.

Making the Financial Blending Process Smoother

Successfully merging finances in a blended family requires strategy, patience, and lots of love. Here are some tips to make the process smoother:

1. **Seek Professional Advice:** Consider seeking advice from financial advisors who specialize in blended families. They can provide you with tailored solutions and guidance.

2. **Have Regular Family Finance Meetings:** Regular family finance meetings can be a platform for discussing money matters, addressing concerns, and making collective decisions.

3. **Patience is Key:** Harmonizing financial matters in a blended family takes time. Don't rush the process and allow your family members time to adjust.

4. **Always Prioritize Love and Respect:** Money matters can be sensitive,

but love and respect should always take precedence. Approach all financial discussions and decisions with this principle in mind.

Blending families and finances is indeed challenging, but it is a journey filled with valuable lessons and opportunities for growth. As you traverse this path, remember that the ultimate goal is to create a financially secure and emotionally nourishing environment for all family members. Your shared love and mutual respect are your most potent tools in this endeavor. Keep communication channels open, navigate financial challenges with empathy, and celebrate every milestone on your journey to financial unity. In this way, you'll build not only a secure financial future but a blended family founded on love, trust, and mutual respect.

9 PLANNING FOR THE GOLDEN YEARS

In the journey of life, retirement is a significant milestone that can signal the start of some of the best years of your life. It's a time for exploration, relaxation, and, most importantly, enjoying the fruits of your years of labor. But to truly enjoy these golden years, careful planning as a couple is crucial.

Creating a Shared Vision

The first step in retirement planning is creating a shared vision for your golden years. This shared vision becomes the compass that guides your financial planning.

1. **Identify Your Retirement Goals:** What do you want your retirement to look like? Do you envision traveling the world, spending time with grandchildren, or pursuing a hobby? Write down your goals and ensure they align with your partner's vision.

2. **Estimate the Cost:** Each goal will carry a cost. Whether it's the expenses for your travel dreams or the amount needed to maintain your desired lifestyle, an accurate estimation can guide your savings and investment strategies.

3. **Discuss Timing:** When do you both plan to retire? Remember, age plays a significant role in determining social security benefits and pension payouts. Moreover, it influences the duration for which your retirement savings need to last.

Understanding Your Current Financial Situation

Before making any future plans, it's crucial to understand where you currently stand financially.

1. **Evaluate Your Assets:** Take stock of all your assets, including savings accounts, investment portfolios, property, and other valuable possessions.

2. **Review Your Debts:** It's equally crucial to have a clear understanding of your liabilities. This includes mortgages, loans, and any other outstanding debts.

3. **Net Worth:** Subtract your total liabilities from your total assets to determine your net worth. This will help you measure your progress and see where you stand in your journey towards financial security.

Determining Your Retirement Income

Retirement income can come from several sources. Identifying these sources can help you anticipate your retirement cash flow and make necessary plans.

1. **Pensions:** If you or your partner have a pension from work, determine how much you can expect to receive and when you can start drawing it.

2. **Social Security Benefits:** Familiarize yourself with how Social Security works. The amount you'll receive depends on your earnings history and the age you start claiming benefits.

3. **Investments and Savings:** These will likely constitute a significant portion of your retirement income. Look at your current investment portfolio, IRAs, and 401(k)s.

4. **Other Sources:** These could be rental income, part-time work, or even a business you might consider starting during your retirement years.

Remember, retirement planning is not a one-time exercise but an ongoing process that requires regular reevaluation and adjustment. However, taking these initial steps will set you firmly on the path to a secure and comfortable retirement. In the next parts of this chapter, we'll delve into understanding pensions and Social Security benefits in more depth and explore effective investment strategies to maximize your retirement savings.

Understanding Pensions and Social Security Benefits

Pensions and Social Security can be significant sources of retirement income. Let's delve deeper into understanding these.

Pensions

Pensions are defined benefit plans where the employer guarantees a set payout upon retirement. The payout amount is typically based on factors such as your years of service, salary, and the plan's specific formula.

1. **Knowing Your Pension Plan:** Understand the specifics of your pension plan. Read through your plan documents, or talk to your HR department to clarify details.

2. **Spousal Benefits:** Some pensions provide benefits for the spouse after the pensioner's death. Understand these benefits and include them in your retirement planning.

3. **Pension Vesting:** Vesting refers to the amount of time you need to work for your company before you have the right to your pension. Know your vesting schedule.

4. **Pension Safety:** Although pensions are generally reliable, company bankruptcy can jeopardize them. Research the financial health of your company and the security of your pension.

Social Security Benefits

Social Security is a federal program that provides benefits to retirees based on their earnings history.

1. **Calculating Your Benefit:** The Social Security Administration (SSA) calculates your benefit based on your 35 highest-earning years. You can use the SSA's online calculator to estimate your benefit.

2. **Choosing When to Claim:** You can start claiming Social Security benefits as early as 62, but the longer you wait (up until age 70), the larger your monthly check will be.

3. **Spousal and Survivor Benefits:** Your spouse may be eligible for benefits based on your work record. If you pass away, your spouse and minor children may also be eligible for survivor benefits.

Both pensions and Social Security provide a steady stream of income during retirement. However, they are rarely enough to cover all your expenses, especially if you have lofty retirement goals. Therefore, savings and investments play an equally crucial role in securing your golden years.

In the final part of this chapter, we will explore effective investment strategies and how to make the most out of your retirement savings. Your golden years are meant to be a time of relaxation and enjoyment. By understanding and optimizing your pension and Social Security benefits, you lay a solid foundation for a comfortable retirement.

Maximizing Your Retirement Savings: Effective Investment Strategies

Apart from pensions and Social Security, your personal savings and investments form the third pillar of your retirement income. This section delves into strategies that can help you grow your nest egg and secure your golden years.

Start Early and Save Consistently

Time is your most significant ally when it comes to investing. Starting early and saving consistently allows you to take advantage of compound interest, where your interest earns more interest. It's never too late to start, and even small amounts can grow over time.

Understanding Your Risk Tolerance

Investing involves risk, and your risk tolerance determines the type of investments you should consider. Typically, younger individuals have a higher risk tolerance and can invest more in stocks, which have the potential for higher returns but also higher volatility. As you approach retirement, it's advisable to shift towards more conservative investments like bonds.

Diversify Your Investments

"Diversify your investments" is a standard piece of financial advice. Spreading your investments across a variety of asset classes like stocks, bonds, and real estate can help reduce risk.

Optimize Your Retirement Accounts

1. **Employer-Sponsored Retirement Plans:** If your employer offers a 401(k) or similar plan, contribute enough to get the maximum employer match, if one is offered. This is essentially free money that can significantly boost your retirement savings.

2. **Individual Retirement Accounts (IRAs):** Traditional and Roth IRAs offer different tax advantages. Contributions to a traditional IRA may be tax-deductible, while withdrawals in retirement are taxed as income. With Roth IRAs, contributions are made with post-tax dollars, but withdrawals in retirement are tax-free.

3. **Health Savings Account (HSA):** If you have a high-deductible health plan, consider contributing to an HSA. These accounts offer triple tax benefits: tax-deductible contributions, tax-free growth, and tax-free withdrawals for eligible medical expenses. Once you turn 65, you can use HSA funds for any purpose, although non-medical withdrawals will be taxed as income.

Regularly Review and Adjust Your Investment Strategy

As you progress towards retirement, your financial situation and goals may change. Regularly reviewing and adjusting your investment strategy helps ensure it stays aligned with your retirement vision.

Working With a Financial Advisor

While it's entirely possible to plan for retirement on your own, working with a financial advisor can be beneficial. They can provide expert advice tailored to your specific situation, help you avoid common pitfalls, and keep you on track towards your retirement goals.

Remember, there's no one-size-fits-all strategy when it comes to retirement planning. Each couple's situation is unique, and the best approach is the one that fits your specific needs and goals.

In closing, retirement planning is about more than just crunching numbers. It's about setting the stage for a period of life that can be incredibly fulfilling and satisfying. By setting clear goals, understanding your current financial situation, determining your potential retirement income, and employing effective investment strategies, you can ensure your golden years are truly golden

10 MONEY AND HAPPINESS - SUSTAINING FINANCIAL AND MARITAL BLISS

Our journey thus far has navigated the intricacies of financial planning as a couple, underscoring the profound impact it has on relationships. As we draw this journey to a close, this final chapter revisits the essence of financial harmony and relationship satisfaction. We delve into how to sustain financial and marital bliss, taking a holistic perspective that goes beyond mere financial strategies.

Understanding the Link Between Money and Happiness

Money in itself does not equate to happiness, but it is a tool that, when used wisely, can contribute to a sense of well-being and security. Understanding this link is the first step in creating and sustaining a harmonious financial life.

1. **Financial Security Over Wealth Accumulation:** Strive for financial security rather than focusing purely on wealth accumulation. Having enough money to meet your needs and pursue your interests can bring a sense of contentment.

2. **Money as a Means, Not an End:** View money as a means to an end and not an end in itself. It's a tool that enables you to live a fulfilling life rather than being the primary goal of life.

3. **Balancing Present and Future Needs:** While planning for the future is crucial, don't forget to live in the present. Balance is key. Allow yourselves small luxuries while maintaining responsible saving and investing habits.

Sustaining a Healthy Money Dialogue

Communication is the backbone of a strong relationship, and money dialogue is no exception. Here's how to keep the conversation healthy:

1. **Regular Money Dates:** Set aside a regular time to discuss finances. Use this time to review your budget, discuss financial goals, and address any concerns.

2. **Stay Open and Honest:** Always be transparent about your financial situation. Honesty fosters trust, a crucial element in any relationship.

3. **Empathetic Listening:** When discussing finances, listen to your partner's concerns and perspectives with empathy. Understanding their viewpoint can lead to more productive conversations.

The Art of Compromise

Financial harmony is not about one partner dictating the rules. It's about finding a middle ground that respects both partners' values and goals.

1. **Shared Decisions:** Major financial decisions should always be made together. This promotes a sense of joint ownership and accountability.

2. **Respecting Individuality:** Despite being a couple, you're still individuals with unique desires and needs. Acknowledge this and allow room for personal spending that doesn't harm your overall financial goals.

Maintaining Financial and Marital Resilience

Life is unpredictable, and financial turbulence is often inevitable. Resilience - both financial and marital - helps you weather these storms.

1. **Emergency Fund:** An emergency fund acts as a financial buffer against unexpected expenses, reducing stress and potential conflict.

2. **Supporting Each Other:** Tough times can strain relationships. Remember, you're a team. Provide emotional support and work together towards solutions.

Conclusion: The Journey Continues

Our exploration of finances in relationships doesn't end here. It's a continuous journey of learning, adapting, and growing together. Money matters, but it's the strength of your relationship that truly counts. By applying the principles and practices we've discussed throughout this book, you'll be well-equipped to navigate the financial landscape as a team.

As we conclude, remember this: couples that save together, stay together, but it's not just about the money. It's about respect, communication, shared dreams, and mutual support. Here's to a future of financial harmony and relationship bliss - your journey towards that future starts now. here.

ABOUT THE AUTHORS

Christian Wolf is a distinguished professional with comprehensive expertise in political science, public finance, and investment management. Currently an investor and financial advisor, he uses his extensive knowledge to assist clients in meeting their financial goals.

Mary Fiorentino is a dynamic professional excelling in both medicine and finance. As a dermatologist and clinic owner, she delivers exceptional medical care to her patients. With a sharp eye for investment opportunities.

Christian and Mary have been happily married for 20 years, blessed with two wonderful sons. Luke, their eldest, is now 15 years old, while Peter, their younger son, is 11 years old.